LONDON

CONTENTS

two of them got numb enough to bag a few pigeons.

Such reverence for the countryside is, of course, a quality of the aristocracy and the upper-middle class. The working classes of London are drawn, instead, to the seaside, where the myths have to do with winkles and jellied eels, donkey rides on the beach, collapsing amusement piers and bingo. On Saturday mornings when the weather is promising, the trains at Waterloo and Victoria fill up early with day-trippers. I joined a group of football enthusiasts one spring day for an excursion to a match between Chelsea and Southampton. They had a rollicking time knocking back six-packs on the train. The discovery, on arrival, that the Southampton side was unwilling to sell them tickets damp-ened no one's spirits. We all spent an hour in the sun surround-ed by two hundred policemen, and when the game was over my friends refreshed themselves by tearing down brick walls and smashing windows on their way back to the railway station for a rollicking ride home.

Day-trippers whose tastes are less inclined to violence find a wistful, pre-war peace on the golden sands or "magical Mablethorpe" and along the promenades of "sunbelievable Eastbourne". Margate's Victorian pier, 1,240 feet long, was picked up by a North Sea gale in 1979 and its timbers flung across the beach like so many soggy chips. But holidaymakers can still hear Val Doonican sing at the Winter Gardens and watch wrestling at the Oval. They can sit on deck-chairs by the sea, sheltered from the wind and the rowdies by the white-chalk cliffs. They can stay overnight, too, in the little hotels on the streets behind the Esplanade that put on tea dances in the afternoons and sing-alongs in the evenings.

Brighton is the place I return to. Something beckons in its marriage of salt air and sleaze. Bed-and-breakfasts line its back streets, where the unemployed hole up for two weeks on the "Costa del Dole". The smell of old grease wafts over the seafront. At the tip of the one rickety pier still open, the white pavilion seems to cry out for paint even when it's just been painted. I have a snapshot of myself sitting in a deck-chair on the pier. The mist has gathered into droplets on the window behind me. I have a pint in one hand and a packet of chips in the other, and my elbow rests on a trash barrel. I'm smiling — at one with nature.

 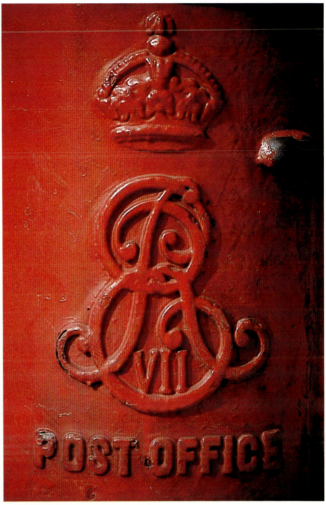

Post Office pillar boxes (above left: the Victoria Regina post-box, and above right: Edward VII post-box) stand firm through many reigns, while Westminster Abbey at right stands firm in the rain. Westminster Abbey has been the crowning-place as well as the burial ground of many of the English monarchs.

Preceding pages: Clockwise, from top left, the Lord Mayor's carriage, a marching member of the Honourable Artillery Company, a Life Guard on horseback, a couple waiting for their bus, a punk in a phone box, a judge in full-bottomed wig, the Lord Mayor during the election and an ostrich-feathered City crier flanked by Pearly Queens.

Left and above, the arrival at the Great Hall of Guildhall of the mace-bearer, and the mace, for the election of the Lord Mayor of the City of London at noon precisely. The occasion is observed with much pomp and ceremony. The Great Hall is also used for public meetings, municipal meetings, state banquets and other City ceremonials.

Preceding pages: St. Paul's Cathedral, against the massed forces of architectural mundanity, rises behind Waterloo Bridge to give the City's dismal skyline a touch of character.

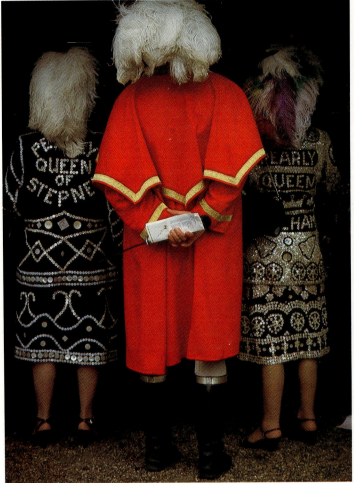

London

Copyright © 1989 Times Editions
1 New Industrial Road, Singapore 1953
All rights reserved for all countries

First published in Great Britain in 1989 by
Planet books, a division of W H Allen & Co Plc,
44 Hill Street, London W1X 8LB

British Library Cataloguing in Publication Data
Newman, Barry
London,
1. London
1. Title
942.1085'8

ISBN 1-85227-056-X

Printed by Tien Wah Press, Singapore
Colour separation by Daiichi, Singapore and Far
East Offset, Malaysia
Typeset by Superskill Graphics, Singapore

LONDON

CITY OF CONTRASTS

Photographs
BERNARD HERMANN

Text
BARRY NEWMAN

W H ALLEN
PLANET

Buckingham Palace, top, the residence of the Queen, takes its name from Buckingham House, built in the 18th century for the Duke of Buckingham. Notice the Royal Standard flying from the roof; it means the Queen is at home. Below, the Royal Family in residence at Madame Tussaud's waxworks, which exhibits life-like wax figures of the famous as well as the infamous. Right, a Life Guard facing a touristic barrage, his breastplate reflecting his headquarters, Horse Guards.

Overleaf: Life Guards in their red tunics and white plumes, and the Royal Horse Guards (or Blues and Royals) on parade. Together, the regiments comprise another item in the Queen's inventory of pageant-makers, the Household Cavalry.

S IN LONDON. 34,

Coca-Cola
REGISTERED TRADE MARK
...refreshing London

Left, black taxi defaced by creeping commercialism. The taxis themselves may soon be supplanted by squared-off cabs that look better suited to Kalgoorlie. Blame it on the Yuppies, seen above, trooping home from the City across the flyover that masquerades as London Bridge. Tower Bridge, in the background has, thankfully, been saved. But, then, it's still under 100 years old.

Preceding pages: A bus crossing the River Thames on Waterloo Bridge, in the lee of St. Paul's, with a message that tells a basic London truth: beneath every busby resides the soul of a punk.

Traffic wardens, above left, lovingly immortalized by the Beatles, add a dash of bright yellow to London. No, not the hat, but a lovely yellow clamp that immobilizes your car until you pay a jolly fat fine. Symbols of the City: above right, a cat and fiddle logo of a financial institution, the Royal Bank of Scotland, and right, the Bank of England and a stockbroker in top hat — not, unfortunately, reinforced to protect the likes of him when the markets crash and interest rates jump over the moon.

A WPC (Woman Police Constable) above, and barrister, left, looking smart. An archetypal image of the British gentleman the bowler hat has almost totally vanished from the London scene; only a few traditional diehards still wear it, like this barrister on the Strand.

Following pages: The Waterloo Bridge, by night, spreads its elegant frame across the River Thames and the skyline of the City.

London Brick

The shoemaker's shop had probably stood there for a century. It was nothing to look at, just a shopworn shopfront in the succession of fruiterers, chemists and newsagents on Old Brompton Road. But the shoemaker was a man of substance. He was no craftsman — he wouldn't have had a chance at Lobb's in St. James's. He simply knew what he was doing, did it well, did it quickly. And he was helpful. It was a quality to treasure in a city where the mood that prevails among shopkeepers, secretaries and civil servants is one of terrible *un*helpfulness. If it hadn't been for that kind man, my briefcase would never have known the taste of Hide Food.

So it was with a pang of loss that I arrived on Old Brompton Road one morning to find the shop and the shoemaker gone. My briefcase had sprung another leak. I was looking forward to a quick stitch. At first, I thought I had walked too far. I doubled back. Then I noticed a place I didn't recall from earlier visits. The lettering on the window was a flat grey, with a thin, grey-pink underline. The door was grey, the knob grey-pink. I walked inside. The carpet was grey and the ceiling was grey. The walls were grey, with a thin grey-pink line where the chair rail should have been. Three dark-grey desks stood on a raised platform along the wall. Each was lit by a spotlight hidden in the ceiling. On each rested a dark-grey computer. And behind each sat a young man in a dark-grey suit.

My shoemaker had been supplanted by the vilest of parasites to breed in London since the Black Death. They were estate agents.

They looked at me blankly when I asked what had happened to the man who could stitch up my briefcase. Yes, said one of them, perhaps there had been a cobbler here at some point. He didn't really know. I walked out, my stomach in a knot, thinking of all the shoemakers and tailors and shirt launderers that have been replaced on every thoroughfare of Central London by these gentrificating merchants of capital gains.

There is a touch of guilt in this. For I am one of those who have fed estate agents' ravenous hoards. I bought a house in Fulham. A hundred years ago, my street was home to the petite bourgeoisie. Later, the houses were cut up into flats. The working class moved in. There are people, old people, on my street who were born in those flats and still live in them. The estate agents, no doubt, stake out their houses — the stonework black with decades of London smoke — and wait to snap them up and sell them off as "stunning, fully-modernized period houses, decorated to highest standard, close to all amenities". A woman who came by to tidy up just after I had moved my family in took one listen to our accents and said, "Americans. It'll be Arabs next."

Like a typhoid carrier, I felt hurt but had to agree. When I came to London, I had expected to live among Londoners. I soon realized that the only Londoners to speak of in Central London live in Nash terraces and drive Daimlers. By an estate agent's sleight of hand I had landed in Earl's Court, the traditional port of call for gullible and cash-short foreigners. The atmosphere there struck me as a combination of Greenwich Village and Times Square, minus the bookshops and the movie houses.

Earl's Court Road is a main truck route to the continent. Shrieking juggernauts crash along it at all hours, past troops of backpackers just in from Perth and Wellington searching for some place to stay on the first night of their Overseas Experience. The streets branching east and west are crowded with launderettes, Ugandan Indian groceries, and bucket shops with signs in their windows advertising cheap flights to Wagga Wagga. Arabs in white robes under woollen suit jackets congregate in the doorways of takeaway kebab houses, waiting for visiting hours to begin at Cromwell Hospital, where the Saudi royals send their less-exalted subjects. The human detritus of distant coups, from Iran to the Philippines, take refuge in bed-and-breakfasts with names like The Hotel Ramses. Then they root themselves in one of ten thousand bedsitters — a furnished room with a gas hob in a paint-poor, four-storey house that has twenty buzzer buttons on the door jamb.

It was in Earl's Court that I first encountered the depths of British tackiness. The burnt-brown shades of London brick became linked in my mind with rising damp, a national institution you must live with to understand. Chintz abounds in this country. I sometimes think the architectural depredations that fill London's bomb sites can only have been planned as monuments to the Third Reich. But nothing summons that sense of imperial decay like the scent of green mould growing on the cold, wet wall of a bedroom in Earl's Court.

London's climate is temperate. It never gets all that cold outside. The only place it gets unbearably cold is inside. Every other country I know in Europe, including balmy Spain, has mastered the fundamentals of central heating. It's been barely twenty years since the British discovered it. But the radiators are still wafer thin, and thermostats too complex to comprehend. Even new houses are built with doors on every room to hold back the draughts. Wall-to-wall carpets have been around for a long time, not as an indication of affluence but as a means of keeping the wind from blowing up through the floorboards. When I was a kid, my family back home in New York had storm windows. My father stacked them in the garage. Every autumn, he'd get out the ladder, unhook the screens and hang up the windows. When I described this to a London friend he was amazed by the elegant simplicity of the procedure. Here, double-glazing involves ponderous sheets of glass installed at colossal cost. Most people don't bother with it. I think they like the cold and the damp. They like keeping the bedroom window open in the dead of winter and waking up with ice on the inside of the glass. It toughens them up. It used to be said that the coldest place on earth was the British bedroom. After my stay in Earl's Court, I had to modify that: the coldest place is the British bathroom.

The only Londoners I could identify with certainty in Earl's Court were the leather boys who frequented the gay pub and the blind accordionist at the entrance to the tube. Thanks to my bathroom, however, I was able to live briefly in posher parts of town. After I caught pneumonia, I moved into a hospital near Marble Arch, just north of Mayfair. The hospital was mercifully warm, and gave me the chance to see how the rich Arabs live. Even in the years of the oil glut, they and recently-escaped Lebanese evidently were the only people who could afford the estate agents in that part of town. Having coughed hard enough in that hospital to give myself a hernia, I gained the chance for a week's stay at another hospital, in St. John's Wood. This district was thick with Americans, and Englishmen up from the country asking them for directions to Lords Cricket Ground. I began to see that the heart of London consists of immigrant ghettos, some rich and some poor.

Rich Londoners bull their way into the rich ghettos, and poor Londoners get shoved into the poor ones. An alien from one country is rarely fond of an alien from another country, and it's hard to find a native Londoner who has a soft spot for any of them.

In the colonies, the British were always open-hearted towards their subjects of other races — and never let them into their clubs. When they brought the West Indians over to help run London Transport in the 1950s, no thought was given to the implications for the homogeneity of the British race. It wasn't until unemployment struck hard that London seemed suddenly overrun by superfluous relics of an empire who had the cheek to consider themselves part of the nation merely because they were born in it. At an upper-class, black-tie dinner party, I once asked the guests to guess how many blacks there were in Britain. Estimates ranged upwards from five million. None of them believed the answer: in a country of fifty-six million, West Indian blacks number 400,000. The rules of the game, to the consternation of many, stop the state from sending them home. But the blacks who didn't make it in are now kept out, and those who did make it in are often kept down.

There's an example of progressive ghetto building in the Tottenham section of north London. It's called Broadwater Farm Estate, a nice, bucolic name. You walk to it along streets of freshly-painted Victorian terraces with little flower gardens beneath their bay windows. Turn a corner, and the farm looms up: tower blocks rising above a blank-walled pedestal that covers a parking lot. Narrow concrete stairways lead up to concrete walkways that take you past a few barred shop windows to steel-doored entry halls. The day I walked through the estate, burned-out cars were overturned in the parking lot. Policemen stood in quiet groups. Residents of Broadwater Farm, nearly all of them black, kept their distance. The night before, a small riot had come and gone.

Whites and blacks do have one thing in common. They have no particular love for Indians. Britain's 1.4 million subcontinentals would have been Margaret Thatcher's most avid fans if her immigration officers didn't humiliate them whenever they set foot in Heathrow Airport. Yet they have shown a nation of shopkeepers how to keep shop. And the permanent fear of racial attack hasn't stopped them from prospering, or from flying in their extended families. The only true Londoners, it's said, are born in the East End within the sound of Bow Bells. But a goodly number of the East End's newborns seem to have parents who were born in Bangladesh. The cockneys have scattered to the suburbs. The Jews, abandoning their sweat shops and synagogues, have established bagel bakeries in Stamford Hill and beyond. There isn't a spice or a sari or a newspaper in Dhaka that you can't get now in Brick Lane.

Like the waves of immigrants that went before them, the Bangladeshis will move on to the garden suburbs to be replaced by yet another eager, hard-working flood of hopefuls who have come to London to seek their fortunes. It's happened already, as a matter of fact, except this time the newcomers weren't motivated by dreams of owning a shop or a little factory. These immigrants arrived in dark-grey suits, fresh out of business school. They dreamed of making their first million in thirty days, working the phones in front of computer screens at the brokerage houses that burst out of the City's staid confines as London grew into the Western world's pivotal centre of aggressive greed. These immigrants dreamed BMWs. They dreamed eurobonds. The Big Bang of deregulation freed the City from its clubby, non-competitive past. Merchant-banking heavies from America and Japan moved in, and the Yuppies arrived in the East End.

They looked suspiciously like estate agents, who migrated eastward themselves at the first smell of money. At enormous cost, the developers refurbished disused docks on the Isle of Dogs to what the advertisements call the "highest standard". Facades of blackened London Brick were sandblasted clean. Bay windows replaced loading bays. And the flats were sold off at prices even more enormous. Then the roaring 80s came to their ignominious end. The eurobond traders suddenly discovered for the first time in their young lives that doing deals can result in a dealer's undoing. Yuppies lost their jobs by the thousands, and the estate agents began to consider renting their slick new offices to shoemakers. I have taken a tour of the Isle of Dogs. It's kind of nice. It's sure to get nicer when the fruiterers and chemists and newsagents move back. When the Arabs take over Fulham, I might move there.

41

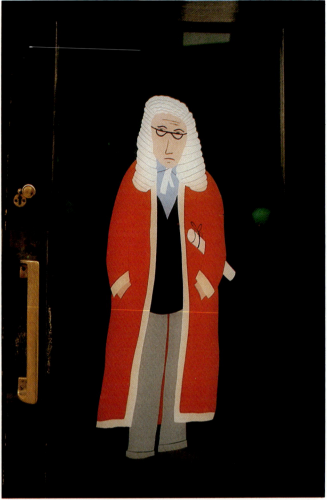

Justice atop Old Bailey, sans blindfold, above left. And a justice decorating the doorway of a nearby bookie, above right. Right, Fleet Street, otherwise known as the "Street of Shame", where the "To Let" signs have gone up as press barons move their shops to high-tech plants in the docklands. Even Dr. Johnson would have a tough time there finding a decent pub.

Preceding pages: London bobbies, nicknamed after their founder Sir Robert Peel, are among the few unarmed police in the world. The London Metropolitan Police, seen here, serve Greater London except for an area called the City of London, which has its own police force. Their predecessors were the famous Bow Street Runners, an enforcement branch, organized in 1749 to catch villains and thieves.

Left, a barrister in wig and soft stock prayerfully crossing The Strand in front of the Law Courts. Above, a private coach doesn't turn heads in this part of town, but TV crews regularly stake out the main entrance of the court's unlikely facade to catch feuding parties en route to the Queen's Bench.

Top, buskers at Camden Lock, picking up a few quid before descending into the tube, where the acoustics, if not the handouts, are far superior. Below, a puppet show at Covent Garden. This fellow keeps his audience amused with his royal puppets. Right, a policeman escorting a punk across the King's Road. The young lady carries a bottle of cider for a good, cheap drink. Policemen are polite to punks, who are almost always harmless.

*Above, Nelson in the midst of a facelift, standing against the azure sky.
The Monument measuring 185 ft high carries a colossal statue of Lord
Nelson who was killed at the Battle of Trafalgar in 1805, where he won
a crucial naval victory over the French. Right, a cabbie who looks like
he could use a new pair of shoes.*

*Following pages: Trafalgar Square, named after Lord Nelson's famous
victory, is the site of the well-known National Gallery and the church of
St. Martin-in-the-Fields. It is a traditional rendezvous for political
rallies, Christmas carolling as well as the ubiquitous pigeons.*

51

A Yeoman Warder, better known as a Beefeater, above, delivering his set speech at the Tower of London while a resident raven takes it in. Notice the Beefeater's costume said to date from the 1500s. The Tower of London, located at the eastern edge of the City, has had a varied past — as a fortress, a royal residence, and a state prison. It is presently maintained as a military garrison. At right, a view of the Ladies with a turret of Tower Bridge in the background.

Big Ben, above, poking its pinnacle from behind Waterloo Bridge. Known for its accuracy the clock is still wound by hand. The name "Big Ben" — named after Sir Benjamin Hall, Commissioner of Works when it was installed in 1859 — originally referred to the 13-ton bell but later came to include the clock itself. Right, a busker of the old school at his regular spot in front of the Earl's Court tube station. He's been there for years and he must make a fortune.

Sensibly Dressed

She had chosen her costume with such precision, her accessories with such accuracy, that I imagined her standing in front of the mirror an hour earlier saying to herself, "Today, I shall be a Sloane."

Now she stood on the platform of the Gloucester Road tube stop, waiting for the train to High Street Kensington. At least half a dozen others similarly decked out waited with her, but none had achieved the desired image with such fidelity. She wore flat, black shoes, dark-blue stockings, a box-pleated skirt, a ruffled blouse with upturned collar, and a string of pearls. Over this, she had put on her Barbour.

A Barbour must be distinguished from a Husky. A Husky is a quilted jacket that looks as if it were made in China before the Chinese turned fashion conscious. It comes in blue, brown and green, though any colour other than green crosses into the realm of the radical. The Queen and people who want to look like her wear Huskies during country-house weekends, with Hermes scarves tied around their heads against the rain. A Barbour, by contrast, is constructed of the kind of heavy-duty cloth the Royal Navy may once have favoured for suits of sails. The coat is dyed countryside green and smeared with at least three pounds of grease. Wearing a Barbour on the Circle Line announces that one has family connections who own large estates and thousands of pheasants, as this young woman no doubt dreamed she did.

To complete the effect, she had pulled her straight blonde hair severely back and tied it with a black velvet ribbon. And to transport the image to new extremes, she carried on her arm a wicker basket. It wasn't filled with daisies, however, and when the train arrived, she failed to skip aboard.

The scientific classification of this specimen is "Sloane Ranger". It means she lives somewhere in the southern stretch of London, west of Westminster and possibly even south of the Thames — but that the centre of her universe, and the universe of her family, is Sloane Square. The male of the species wears a blue pin-striped suit, striped shirt, polka-dot tie, heavy brogues on his feet and a wooden-handled umbrella over his arm. On the tube, he talks loudly with his chums while on his way to work at a job his uncle got him in the City. Like Londoners of every stripe (and polka dot) he wears his class and his politics on his sleeve.

In any city, foreigners are easy enough to spot. I can make the distinction now between the Dutch (could it be their ankle boots?) and the Spanish (something to do with shoulder pads). I can finger an American at fifty yards: Reeboks, Burberry trench coat, Burberry hat, and a stiffness in the stance reminiscent of old Ben-Gay commercials. But in how many other cities can you tell by the way a person dresses and combs his hair not just his income and his class, but which wing he favours of which political party? A hard-left Labourite, I've decided, has a shorter, tamer hairdo than the bleeding hearts to his right. A Tory "wet" wears his hair wilder than the Thatcherite. A Liberal who favoured a merger with the Social Democrats will get on the tube in a sports jacket.

To someone fresh off the planes from Paris or Rome, or Munich for that matter, the striking thing about the Londoner is his all-round clunkiness. That can be explained by the way young upper-working and middle-middle class women in white blouses and snug black skirts trip and clatter along the sidewalks, having armed the tips of their spike-heeled shoes with drawing-pins. Their boyfriends contribute to the effect by setting off their light-grey suits with bright-pink ties and wearing socks that droop and bunch around the ankles. You can tell what audience a television news show aims at by the brightness of the presenter's ties. A glimpse at their socks would surely served the same end.

I lay responsibility for the respectable upper-working-middle-middle London look at the automatic doors of Marks and Spencer, genius purveyors of things clunky to the British body politic. On the expanse of a Marks and Sparks shopping floor, you'll find all the accoutrements that make this the land of the sensibly dressed: sturdy tweeds, flat caps, and those comfy slippers and cardigans made for sitting by the gas fire on a wet afternoon. You'll find the same durable duffle coat that Michael Foot, former leader of the Labour Party, gave new fame when he wore it to place a wreath at the Cenotaph on Remembrance Day. And you'll find rack after rack of frilly, slinky ladies' undergarments that cater matter-of-factly to one of the country's weirder sartorial obsessions.

Outside underwear, Marks and Spencer has undergone a

subtle and possibly subversive change of late. Although my slippers remain in abundance, it has become difficult to locate my standard-issue pullovers in the jumper bins. Now they come in lunatic cuts and colours that scream pernicious modernity. If blame for London clunk can be laid at the doorstep of Marks and Spencer, blame for the trendification of Marks and Spencer might well be laid at the doorstep of Kensington Palace, wherein resides the ultimate Sloane, Her Royal Highness the Princess of Wales.

She was a pudgy, pouting kindergarten teacher before she married Prince Charles in 1981. At 20, Lady Diana Spencer (no relation to Marks) hadn't managed to pass a single exam required by British schools for the equivalent of an American high-school diploma. "Gentlemen," the press was told, "she has no past." But did she ever have a future. After watching her carried to the altar at St. Paul's like some sacrificial virgin, the British turned her into a twentieth-century fertility goddess. She responded by losing an unhealthy amount of weight and becoming a manne-quin, all for the greater glory of the London rag trade.

Day after tiresome day, her image appears on the front of the tabloids, swaddled in yet another glittering designer creation equal in cost to the annual deficit of Lambeth Borough Council. But don't think for a minute that the Princess offends anyone besides the stalwarts of the loony left. She has, in fact, transcended class-bound Sloane Rangerdom. And she has surpassed the rest of the Royal Family in grasping the House of Windsor's secret of successful monarchy: that to be truly upper class, one must be truly low-brow.

For the shoppers at Marks and Spencer, Princess Diana has cued a costume change. Joan Collins couldn't do as much, though costume changes are hardly unknown to London. The Queen does it every time she picks up the sceptre. Britons may wear their class on their Harris tweeds, but they also share a classless and not-too-classy giddiness about dressing up. It would be tough to find a British comic who didn't keep a drag outfit in his truck. A favourite on the telly is a show called *Come Dancing*, an amateur competition in which young men in tightly-cut tuxedos spin around a ballroom trundling young women dressed as banana splits. I have an upper-class friend who revels in suiting up to look like an American flag whenever he comes over for dinner.

As in no other city, with the possible exception of Delhi, the streets of London teem with people who appear to be on their way to masquerade parties. It is nothing at all to buy an almond danish in a bakery on the Strand from a shop assistant with pink hair and a ring in her nose. It is just as common to see a man emerge from the Law Courts across the street in a silk gown, a soft stock and a horsehair wig. Whether it's the Chelsea Pensioners' Cheese Ceremony or Doggett's Coat and Badge Race, Londoners will always find an excuse to pull on their miniver robes and Tudor bonnets, their ribbons and their plumes. The Royals, thanks to a theatrical nineteenth-century effort to popularize the monarchy, have nearly as many uniforms and decorations as Imelda Marcos had shoes. For them, regalia is a suited-up statement of British history's most important fact — that Britain has been around for an awfully long time.

The full-dress store in the Household Cavalry's Hyde Park barracks differs only in detail from the dressing rooms of the Royal Ballet during a production of the Sleeping Beauty. Corporal of Horse, Steven Hyatt, a Queen's trumpeter turned military property master, once showed me around the place. It blazed with official finery: silver helmets with enamelled crests and yak-hair plumes, scarlet tunics, polished breastplates, horse blankets embroidered in silver and gold with the battle honours of Balaklava and Waterloo. In a place of honour hung a trumpeter's coat of purple velvet covered with bands of gold lace. This was Cpl. Hyatt's coat. He wore it with white buckskin breeches, patent-leather jackboots and a royal-blue riding helmet — the racing colors of Charles II.

"I put it on for Prince Charles' wedding, the Queen's Jubilee, Trooping the Colour," Cpl. Hyatt told me. "There's an excitement. You just can't explain the feeling you get. That's why I joined, really — to wear all this sort of snuff and get paid. These punks walking around on the street, they don't get paid for it, do they?"

Well, not exactly. The cults of working-class youth are, on the face of it, the flip side of London pageantry, thumbing their clothes at the rituals of state. Today's young have gone the limit: they are nearly as flamboyant as the Lord Chief Justice. There are punks with rainbow-striped hair, skinheads with no hair at all, and something called a bonehead, which is a skinhead with tattoos on his face. These kids don't dress to kill, merely to frighten. If regalia celebrates Britain's longevity, the gruesome gear of punks and skinheads might be seen as a bitter jape at the country's decline.

In the mid 1970s, when the first punk stuck a safety pin through his nose, the semioticists went wild. They took every new punk accessory as another symbol of societal angst. But by the time the cosmetic companies started flogging pastel hair dye and super-stick gel, punk was long dead. It had been usurped, like the counter-culture before it, by the high-powered designers of Chelsea and the knock-off artists of Oxford Street. I once met a young woman who was standing behind the counter of a stall in a King's Road clothing emporium. She sold fashions of her own design, and this is what she looked like: the sides of her head were shaved to a couple of inches above her ears; the hair on top, dyed hay yellow, stood straight up; her eyebrows were shaved off; there was a wavy line of blue and gold across her forehead; her lips were lavender, outlined in dark blue and daubed with gold. And here is what she wore: a black crucifix suspended from an ear lobe; cowbells and plastic pearls around her neck; a goat-hair yoke across her shoulders; a black-mesh cowl under the yoke; a white muslin dress under the cowl, and two steel-studded, black leather belts around her waist. On the shelves behind her were her creations. Breast plates. Polished breast plates, not much different from the ones I saw in the Household Cavalry's full-dress store. "I'm into armour," the young woman told me. In London, armour is the usual thing.

Maybe that's why punk has refused to go away. Too bizzare for Londoners to disregard, it has become another variant of fancy dress. On any Friday evening, an hour or two after the work day ends, normally clunky people transform themselves into weekend punks. All it takes is a quick rinse, an all-black ensemble, a couple of studded belts, some fingernail glitter, and a thick smear of deep-purple lipstick. I expect someone will soon come out with a reversible Barbour, lined in black. The most outlandish full-time punks left in London lounge around the fountain in Trafalgar Square, amid the pigeons and the tourists — who are often one and the same. When tourists come up and ask to take their pictures, they nod, pose, and charge a pound. "Most punks in London do it," one once told me. "Some days you can pick up thirty quid at the Tower." It seems an ideal occupation for anyone who gets a kick out of dressing up. Corporal of Horse Hyatt might reconsider his choice of career.

A band concert at St. James's Park, right, during a workday lunchtime. Tourists rent the deck-chairs while Londoners stretch out on the grass, more typically in singlet and with trousers rolled for a calf tan. A squirrel perched on a tree meanwhile enjoys a bite and the scene.

Preceding pages 62-63: Last night of the Proms, the annual summer bash at the Albert Hall where Sloane Rangers and tourists wrap themselves in the Union Jack and listen to the classics. If you don't like sitting on the floor, it's easier to watch it on the telly.

64-65: Swan Lake at the Royal Opera House, Covent Garden.

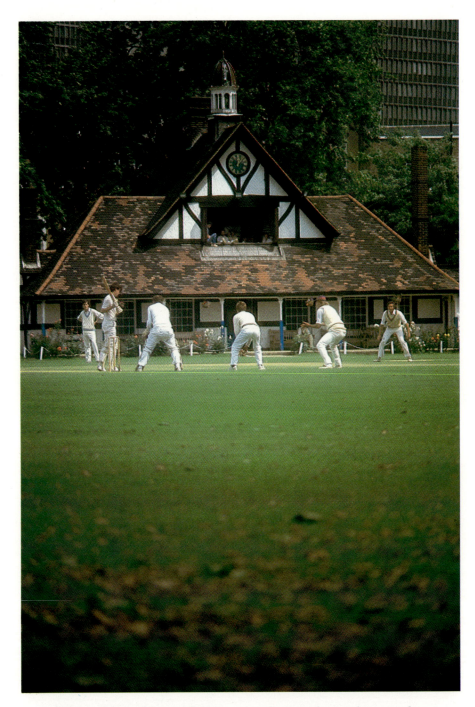

Above, cricket at Vincent Square, once a bear garden, and now used as playing fields. Right, on his way to cut a ribbon in Battersea Park, the Prince of Wales engages in tall talk.

Following pages: Three genteel games — bowling at the Muswell Hill Bowling Club, croquet at the Hurlingham Club in gentrifying Fulham, and cricket at Lord's Cricket Ground in St. John's Wood. A nice way to spend a summer's day.

Left, a horse show at Clapham Common. The young lady on the left isn't kidding around; she's a pro and so is the owner who pays her to ride his horse. Above, a tic tac man at the races, telegraphing the odds to his bookie without the aid of computer.

*Regent's Park, above, has a zoo (London's biggest and most famous). Hyde
Park, right, doesn't. It has Speakers' Corner, located in the park's
north-eastern corner near Marble Arch, where free speech reigns (on Sundays)
in defiance of the Official Secrets Act.*

Pearlies adorned with medals and pearl buttons arrive at St. Martin-in-the-Fields in Trafalgar Square for a special service. So does the dog.

Preceding pages: Pearlies trekking across Westminster Bridge, doing their bit for charity, for which they are well-known. The original East Enders, every one of them is either a king, a queen or an heir apparent.

Pearlies on the South Bank. If you don't happen to catch them in such profusion on the street, there's one place where you're almost sure to find them come Sunday afternoon: the City of London Museum.

Following pages: A Pearly King and his accordion playing, no doubt, an old Music Hall song. And right, an honest East End pub which besides serving the usual pint of bitter may offer juke-box music, billiards, darts and even video games. The pubs — and London has well over 5,000 pubs — are a unique institution of British life.

The South Bank pub, like the umbrella in the foreground, is an enduring symbol of London. From Victorian to high-tech the pubs offer a wide variety of food ranging from the traditional roast beef and steak and kidney pudding to anglicized version of nouvelle cuisine. Besides serving as eating places, the pubs are frequented by Londoners who go there for an evening of convivial chat, sing-a-longs or even a game of darts or billiards.

Following pages: Tower Bridge looking east, towards the abandoned wharfs downriver. Built of steel with a cladding of stone to match the facade of the medieval Tower of London behind it the bridge is widely recognised as a symbol of London. Few ships come here nowadays, the only ship that ties up this side of the bridge of late is the floating museum, HMS Belfast, a famous British cruiser during World War II.

They Are What They Eat

Walk down Farringdon Road, past the Guardian, past the antique shops, past the Morning Star in its Marxist decay, and you'll soon arrive at the portals of The Quality Chop House. When I first went there, with a friend who guaranteed a great find, I somehow got it into my head that the place was called "The Workingman's Cafe" — cafe pronounced the English way, like "caff". The window threw me off. It's milky on the bottom, and has a ribbon of red about face high. Along the ribbon, the following is inscribed: "Progressive working-class caterer." On the pavement in front of the window stands a placard on struts, something you might expect a man to wear as a sandwich-board if the Chop House ever wanted to advertise. It lists its newspaper reviews, including one from 1974, and alleges that inside one can order "the best cup of tea in London". Well, you have to go in.

The room is long and deep. Along both walls are booths with high, dark-wood backs. The benches are narrow and the fit tight between their backs and the long tables, polished by a century of waitresses wiping off the bacon drippings as they say, "What'll ya have, luv?" A few years ago, at lunchtime, the Quality was crowded. You squeezed into the booth alone at 12:45, and by one o'clock you had to share it with four navvies off a road gang. But I hear the place has changed hands, and that might explain why the crowds are down, and why the calendars with pictures of naked ladies have been replaced by those old, hand-coloured book illustrations they sell in Cecil Court. But the food — the food is the same solid, honest English cafe food that helped build the empire, and has given Britain one of the highest rates of heart disease the world has ever known.

On my inaugural voyage to London, in 1968, I went to a cafe. I didn't know then that it was the epitome of British gastronomy; I know now. Looking around at what the others were eating I ordered a combination plate that seemed to be the house speciality: sausage and egg and beans and chips, with two slices of buttered white bread. A memorable meal. The only exotic food I ate on that trip was just about the only exotic food you could find in London

— Indian. I recall eating the meat "Vindaloo" at an Indian restaurant in Hampstead and gagging on the chili as the waiters giggled. I longed for a plate of spaghetti, but spaghetti hadn't come to London yet.

It arrived after Britain joined the Common Market and the Channel was no longer able to hold back the tide of pasta. Today, spaghetti abounds in London. A place near my house in Fulham, "Pizza the Action", serves a serviceable Marguerita. Cypriots run the Greek restaurants, though I can't help but feel that the retsina and the mezes taste better when consumed beneath a canopy with a view of the hot, blue Aegean. The sun's white light does not shine on Charlotte Street. The French have presided over an outbreak of "brasseries", where waitresses and waiters alike wear black vests and long, white aprons. The Turks are here, too, and the Poles and the Hungarians. The hamburger at Joe Allen's rivals the one Joe Allen serves on West 46th Street, though I did eat at another American place once where the corn-on-the-cob came out of a can. The package tour has carried the British so far afield that almost nothing fazes the Londoner anymore. The one cuisine that hasn't caught on is the Spanish. I know of only two tapa bars in London, and one of them brings cappuccino when you ask for cafe con leche. Six million Britons descend on the Costa del Sol in a year, but they evidently steer clear of the gazpacho and eat what the Spanish offer: sausage and egg and beans and chips.

In the splendour of Benidorm, the fare must taste even more awful than it does when you eat it in a London pub. Mahogany partitions, acid-etched glass, tulip lamps, bronze figurines, plush velvet banquettes, mirrors and marble-topped tables surely qualify the pubs of London as the most lavish imaginable emporiums in which to eat the most unimaginably appalling food.

When wholesomeness was reborn, after London stopped swinging in the early 70s, a consumers' movement appeared in Britain known as the Campaign for Real Ale. A thousand beers are brewed in the country, called things like "Old Peculiar" and "Oh Be Joyful!" but until the campaign built up strength many had been co-opted by conglomerates that filtered them, pasteurized them, and artificially fizzed them until they became, as drinkers in London will tell you, "nothing but piss and wind". By the late 70s, beer had been saved. The rattiest pub in London today has a porcelain beer-pull and a couple of deep amber, naturally-carbonated real ales in the cellar. That battle won, innocents like myself awaited the start of the next campaign — the one for real food. As Egon Ronay's pub guides came off the presses, hopes rose. Yet Londoners, who could remember the joys of drinkable ale, had no such recollections when it came to food. In a few pubs, the turkey has become less crumbly, and a slab of brie has appeared beside the block of cheddar in the cold counter. One pub I know serves duck à l'orange, but an Irishman owns it. In most others, the choice hasn't changed and probably won't: shepherd's pie with watery mince oozing beneath the mashed potatoes, wizened-skinned sausages, yecch-yellow curry, and steak and kidney pie that has formed a waxen carapace of grease under the heat lamp. I think I'm going to be ill.

It isn't as if the British lack the raw materials of a grand cuisine. Butchers take a finicky pride in the produce of their lusher places, hanging dead rabbits in the windows of their shops for all to admire. They display the lovely plumage of the season's least fortunate pheasants long enough for the birds to rot and fall into the sawdust; that means they're ready to cook. Up north, working-class men devote large chunks of their lives to the nurture of giant leeks. Londoners don't go that far in public, but this is nevertheless the one city I know where vegetable sellers are so protective of their peppers and tomatoes that they refuse the customer his inalienable right to pick and squeeze. In the Leather Lane street market I once committed the cultural gaffe of choosing a half-dozen peaches for myself. The man behind the pushcart grabbed them out of my hands and flung them back onto the pile, an act which almost certainly is a criminal offence in France. It wasn't fair to the other customers, he told me in a storm of anti-Yank abuse. I presumed this meant he wanted to distribute the rotten ones equally among us.

The British don't really go horribly wrong, when it comes to food, until they set foot in a kitchen. This is where you learn that excellent Scottish beef, pulverized into mince, turns grey under the broiler. This is where the best smoked salmon in the world is slapped onto a plate with a wedge of lemon. No cream cheese. No bagels. What's a New Yorker to make of that?

"No!" screams Emily, my daughter. "I will not have school dinners one more time!"

She goes to a state school, which means the government runs it, as opposed to a public school, which is where the people go who end up running the government. At my daughter's school, a raucous band of designer-socialists labours to transform the "vegetable mush" and "soggy meaty stuff" my daughter hates into creatively unadulterated and hormonally holistic vegetable mush and soggy meaty stuff. They lobby, with no apparent effect, to oust white bread in favour of whole-grain granary loaf, and to install kiwi fruit where "purple crumble with bleach custard" now stands firm. What these good egalitarians don't seem to realize is that school dinners may be the great leveller of British life.

In the London pub, the class barriers that once walled off the public bar from the lounge bar have all but vanished, more in the interest of cash flow, I suspect, than social mobility. Until recently, my own backstreet local had a public bar. Nicotine-tinted lino covered the floor, only a shade darker than the nicotine-stained ceiling. The comforts consisted of one wobbly Formica table with three broken chairs. A dartboard hung on the wall and the crowd hung around it. A doorway led into a back room where young men prowled around two coin-operated snooker tables. The bar itself stood between the public bar and the lounge bar. You couldn't get from one to the other unless you walked outside and went in through another door. The lounge bar had soft seats and the beer cost more. The last time I went to my local, the public bar had disappeared. Now the whole place is one big, plush, carpeted lounge bar. The snooker room has become the "family room". And the beer costs even more.

The object of this upheaval was not, be assured, to elevate the working class, but to woo the trendified middle class away from the wine bars. A wine bar serves a posher calibre of pub food, and it serves wine, just wine. You can't get a beer in a wine bar. The advent of the wine bar made it possible for the higher orders to guzzle Chateauneuf du Pape in peace while the beer-swilling yobbos remained prisoners of their pubs. Recently, a frightening innovation has hit London. A few new places are serving good wine and good beer from the same bar. It's too early to tell if they will survive, but these "salons" make a powerful effort to evade the class issue. They hang rock-video screens from their ceilings, averting all gazes from unacceptable bone structure, and blast the music so loudly that nobody can identify anybody else's accent.

But the upper middles, the aristocracy and the bedrock working class refrain from such daring indulgences. They seek comfort in school dinners. The fare in the refectory of a public school in Westminster differs only marginally from what's on offer at a comprehensive school in Hackney Wick. Like the British tea ceremony, the collective memory of toad-in-the-hole must help unify the nation in times of culinary onslaughts from across the Channel. Schoolboys grow up to eat spotted dick at the Wig and Pen Club and at The Quality Chop House, too. At a long table in their dining room at the Palace of Westminster, their noble lordships tuck into bubble-and-squeak in the honourable company of their peers. A while back, the naughty nostalgia the British harbour for their lost innocence was brought to life in a restaurant that called itself School Dinners. The waitresses wore gym slips and smacked your hand if you didn't finish your spinach.

"Make me a sandwich, please!" screams my daughter, and I hardly blame her.

The British, goes the story, invented the sandwich. Alas, it was just another of those inventions, like the brain scanner, that they failed to develop. When the taste of take-outs improves dramatically between London and a place like Warsaw, where the hot dogs surpass all competitors, something is deeply wrong. Anyone who arrives in London from a sandwich-savvy city tells the same story. You ask the man behind the counter for a ham and cheese, and he replies incredulously: "On the *same* sandwich?" I made my daughter an elaborate New York combo one day, and she came home begging me never to do it again; her friends had ridiculed it in the schoolyard.

Yet I sense a new era on its way. It has long been possible in London to eat a rather thin corned-beef on rather too-soft rye. But in the space of only six years, since I moved here, the pickles have got better. Today, there is a place in this city that will make you an avocado and bacon sandwich with the indifference most shops reserve for chicken on white. And up on Theobold's Road, another place has opened that will not only make a ham and cheese on demand, but will make it with *Swiss* cheese. Nothing else will matter once the sandwich comes to London. Then, I could stay forever.

Horse Guards trotting home in the rain to their headquarters at Whitehall.
They protect the Head of State, who is also the head of the state Church, from the
doubters, from the fundamentalist on the street to the Rastafarian on the bus.

Memories of the Raj. Top, the idealization of empire carved at the base of the Victoria and Albert Memorial in Kensington Gardens. One of London's most remarkable relics, this Victorian Gothic monument is graced by 175 sculpted figures. Bottom, a Punjabi dancer in Holland Park and right, saris floating past the Queen's front door add a splash of colour to the otherwise drab background.

Following pages: Asians doing their bit: taking taxis, reading The Guardian, *getting married and volunteering as an auxiliary policeman.*

NO SMOKING

Despite the value of a Travelcard, there's still the oc

LONDON &

Above, the Queen from the window of her royal Rolls surveys the scene. London today is very much a cosmopolitan and multiracial city with about a million immigrants, mainly from the Commonwealth countries, living in and around central London. They have produced a great cultural and vibrant mix reflected in the many ethnic restaurants, places of worship and in the many service industries that have sprung up in several parts of London.

Preceding pages: For all the talk of eccentricity, London doesn't like eccentrics. Conformity is required, and quiet decorum, when one rides the tube. The Indian boy got the message, and wears his uniform.

Sunday on Petticoat Lane. One of London's more popular tourist attractions, Petticoat Lane gets its name from the many clothes stalls located there. It used to be a traditional Jewish trading area but the Indians are also making their presence felt.

Muslims worshipping at the Sufi Mosque in Shepherd's Bush, left, and in the Great Mosque near Lord's Cricket Ground, top. Shoes and other footwear are removed as a matter of propriety. Bottom, a Muslim book at the British Museum on Great Russell Street.

A Hindu temple in the East End, right, and a musician who plays there, above. The struggle against assimilation isn't what it is in America. The British make it easy. They do their best to help aliens stick to themselves.

Above, Arab ladies shopping in Shepherd's Bush. The least comprehensible, yet the most welcome of outsiders; they're rich, and they have every intention of going home.

Following double-page: Portobello Road during the Notting Hill Carnival. A two-day Afro-Caribbean festival that turns the streets around Portobello Road and Notting Hill into a parade of floats, dancing and music with lots to eat and drink.

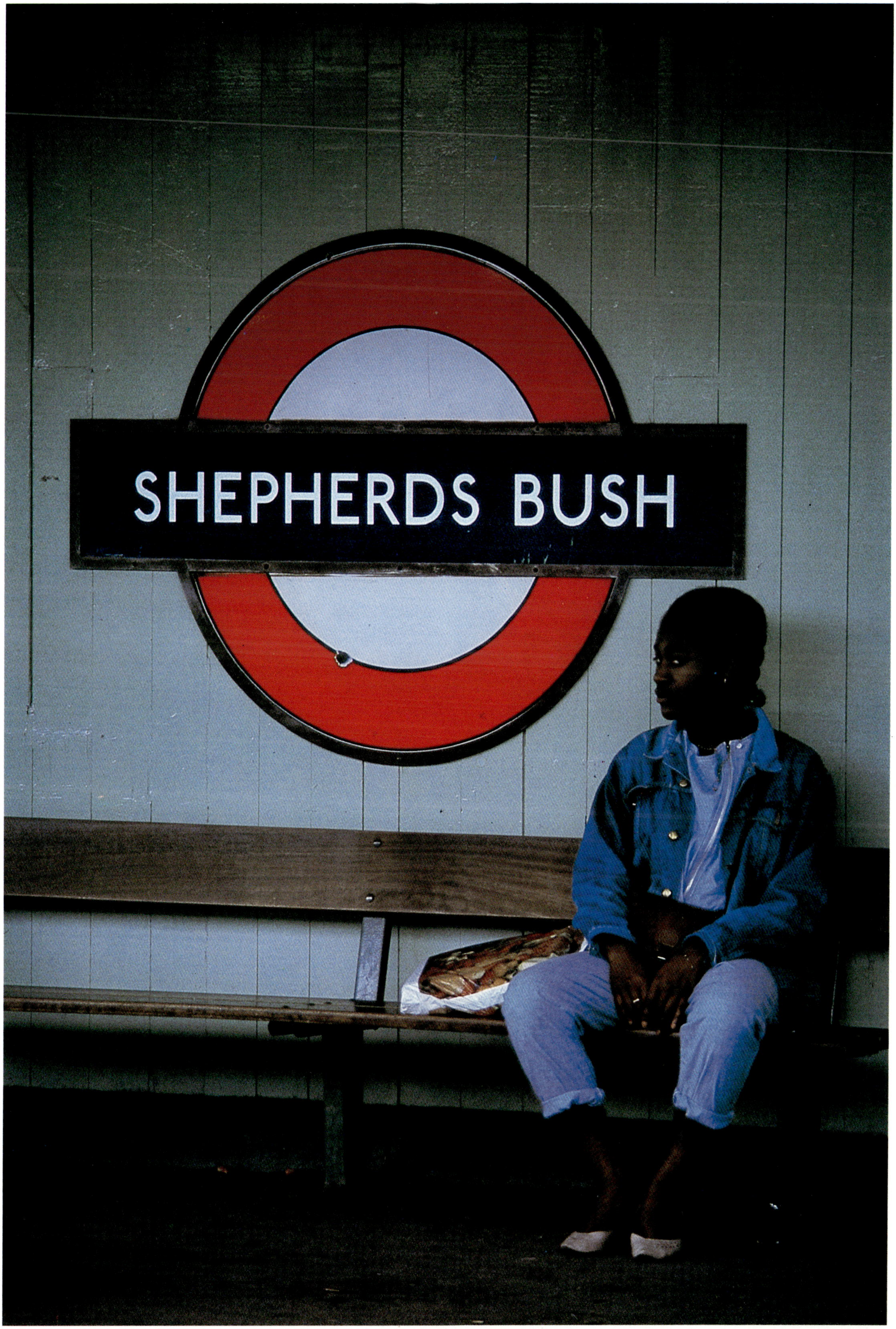
SHEPHERDS BUSH

Above, bebop in Covent Garden, the Royal Opera House of busking, by invitation only. It is the only place in London where busking is legal. Right, Grenada Shortneys, dressed up for their annual carnival celebrations.

A photographer's shop in Brixton Market on Electric Avenue, above, and its owner, right, in his upbeat colourful gear. Established in the 1880s the market now serves a predominantly large West Indian community.

Following double-page: Tourists at St. James's Palace. Built by Henry VIII St. James's was the main royal residence in London for more than a century. It now houses the Lord Chamberlain's office besides serving as the headquarters of the Gentlemen at Arms and the Yeomen of the Guard.

The Centre

The biggest, most sophisticated, most confusing cities — Paris, New York, even Moscow — possess a centre of gravity, some point of focus which draws lightning and emits light: a building called City Hall, perhaps, with a flesh-and-blood mayor in residence whose picture is always in the papers and who shakes hands in the parks on Sunday afternoons. They have football teams, with the city's name stitched across their jerseys, that fly out to do battle in alien burgs. They have bumper stickers.

But not London. This city started out as a network of villages and remains one. The only people I know who call themselves Londoners are cockneys from the City of London. But hardly a cockney, or anybody else, actually lives in the City anymore. The City has a Lord Mayor, who gets pulled around the square-mile in a horse-drawn coach once a year and who doesn't seem to do very much else. And the City has a lot of offices. That's it. The real London is a great plain, covering 610 of those square miles, encompassing thirty-two boroughs, from Hillingdon to Havering, and some 6.7 million people. Race, class, politics, geography and a studiously fragmented system of government keep them from having much of anything to do with one another.

For twenty-two years, until 1986, London did have a government of sorts. It was called the Greater London Council, and it occupied the huge old headquarters of another defunct government, the London County Council, on the south bank of the Thames directly opposite the Palace of Westminster. The GLC took care of the big roads, public housing, town planning. In 1981, with the election of Ken Livingstone as its leader, it tried playing old-fashioned ward politics on a grand scale. Livingstone was hard-left, a builder of minority coalitions against patrician power. He saved Covent Garden for mime artists and purveyors of advanced kitchen implements. He dished out grants to interest groups that all seemed to have names like Black Lesbian Alcoholics United to Smash Blood Sports. Thatcher tired of this. Her government put through a law and abolished the GLC. Livingstone himself was out of a job and London lost its lightning rod.

Yet London didn't mourn, no more than it clung to its red

phone boxes, torn up and carted off to the auction rooms by a privatized and newly-logoed British Telecom. This is a city where local television news shows take all of five minutes and rarely rate a film crew, where local newspapers aren't worth the price even when they're given away free. Quality television and serious newspapers look to the nation, and so does the city. That is the secret of London's identity. It doesn't need a centre because it *is* the centre. Its suburbs don't stop at the green belt. They take in Gwent and Fife and County Down. No longer imperial, London remains imperious. The Queen — opening Parliament, Trooping the Colour — rules ceremoniously. But those who govern make no show of it. They guide the country subtly, according to the precepts of Victorian charity: we know what's best; anyone who feels the need to ask questions has no business having the answers.

Like Downing Street itself, an unpretentious row of town houses, official London can seem disarmingly accessible. On my first visit there, it must have been during the Falkland's war, the street had been closed off by a few police barricades. I showed my press card and walked through. There was the bobby in front of Number 10. I showed him my card, but he had no interest in it. "Knock on the door," he said. I knocked. It opened, and a shirtsleeved officer let me in. I don't know what it's like getting into the White House these days, but I suspect it's different.

Inside, I stood in the foyer a while, admiring the flowers on the mantle, and then joined a few of my colleagues in a green-carpeted back office for an audience with Bernard Ingham, the Prime Minister's Press Secretary. All the reporters were American; in deference to its great ally, the British government grants us special briefings. In deference to Britain's old school ties, we all make believe the briefings never happen. It's our complicity in a closed and condescending system of information control that, in my experience, lands Britain near the bottom of the international *glasnost* league. This country has no Freedom of Information Act. What it does have is the Official Secrets Act, which explicitly forbids any civil servant to say anything about anything to anybody. Those few who break the rules (when the government doesn't put them up to it) get arrested.

Only the doings in Parliament itself offer the British public any hint at the workings of official London. On the basis of that, it must seem to many as if the making of law and policy is a natural outgrowth of public school tomfoolery. Few, if any of the British prime ministers deign to give press conferences. Twice a week, though, he or she faces the government's most vociferous enemies in the uproar of Question Time. The loud barracking that usually interrupts the answers comes across as one of the more hilarious, and pitiful, excuses for open government yet conceived.

For nearly twenty years, this noise has been carried by radio to quiet hamlets up and down the country, reinforcing everyone's certainty that politicians are all cuckoo. Luckily for the politicians, nobody can see them. If they could, it might alter the public image of such respected personages as Denis Healey, the shadow foreign secretary, whose reverberations rise above the roar as he sits red-faced on the Labour front bench bellowing, "Answer the question!" Television has tried for years to set up cameras in the House of Commons. The Commoners wouldn't hear of it, until 1988. A couple of years earlier, back, though, their noble lordships at the other end of the palace did let television in. The atmosphere of their chamber, with its dark-panelled walls and red leather benches softly lit by candelabra, induces sleep rather than high drama. Watching the House of Lords on television remained captivating for about a day, and then everyone switched back to *Gardeners' World*. Just as well. Their lordships toil quietly on, examining and amending the torrent of bills rashly passed in "the other place". Such trifles as the media and elections have never impeded them from acting in the best interests of democracy.

It is possible, sitting in the Lords' gallery on a somnolent afternoon, to believe for a moment that you know what this country and the city at its heart are about. But the feeling never lasts. I sometimes think the only creatures confident in their grasp of London's dimensions are the tourists. They chart their course, maps in hand, down King's Road, around the Serpentine, past Buckingham Palace, along the Mall, through Admiralty Arch to Westminster Abbey and onwards to St. Paul's and The Tower. They buy their deerstalkers at Harrods, have a pint in a pub and tea at Claridge's. They do the British Museum, see a Soho strip show, take a day trip to Hampton Court. After five days, they understand London. And they take home a jar of marmalade from Fortnum and Mason to prove it.

Top left, the Lord Chief Justice in ceremonial robes and wig at the Royal Courts of Justice in the Strand. Top right, the statue of Queen Anne in state robes surveys the all-Service service at the right as the Queen emerges on the step of St. Paul's with an ermined Lord Mayor.

Preceding pages: The Queen's Bodyguard of the Yeomen of the Guard on their way to their annual inspection by the Queen at Buckingham Palace.

Princess Diana, coyly dejected in her sailor suit while those around her get to wear the really fun uniforms. But the Grenadier Guardsman, right, shows it isn't so much fun when you change into khakis; the medal is awarded for doing time in Britain's Gaza Strip.

Following double-page: Sports clothes, at Royal Ascot (above), in St. James's Park (below), and on Rotten Row in Hyde Park (right) with the Morgan Society. It's hard to tell who gets the most exercise — the punters, the players, the horses, or the tailors.

Above, the Queen arrives at Ascot with Prince Philip, who would much prefer to be driving a carriage, in a competition, than riding in one. The woman at the right belongs to the most populous herd at these races. She's a clothes horse.

Following double-page: Ascot winners' enclosure. The main event is the Ascot Gold Cup, a 2½-mile race run by horses above three years old.

134

A young lady in a boater gets an award from Prince Andrew for boating at the Henley Royal Regatta. Established in 1839, the regatta is an annual event held on the River Thames at Henley-on-Thames.

Preceding pages: At the Henley Regatta — the Sloane Ranger's favourite day trip.

H. M. and Prince Charles at a polo game at Smith's lawn, Windsor. The oldest of equestrian sports, polo became popular in England after its introduction by the military. The game attracted thousands of spectators with matches played at Richmond Park, Windsor Great Park and Hurlingham.

*Above, left and preceding pages: Garden Party at Buckingham Palace,
where adoring throngs pile in a few times a year for a moment of chit chat
with the Windsors. The Queen is in yellow talking to a lady in a green hat
who seems to have jumped the queue. Like all royal duties, garden parties
are hard work.*

The Yeoman of the Guard, above, go home after their inspection, and so do the Queen and the Duke of Edinburgh after a hard day's work. The Yeomen of the Guard — not to be confused with the Yeomen Warders of the Tower of London who are similarly dressed in Tudor costume — are specially chosen from the Army, the Marines and the Royal Air Force.

After Trooping the Colour, royals and sergeant majors, wait for the "flypast", over the Palace, the RAF's annual reenactment of the Blitz. The Queen usually appears with the rest of her family on this occasion on the balcony of Buckingham Palace, still in uniform.

Preceding pages: The King's Troop, Royal Horse Artillery. Yes, the King's Troop. The Queen decided not to change the name.

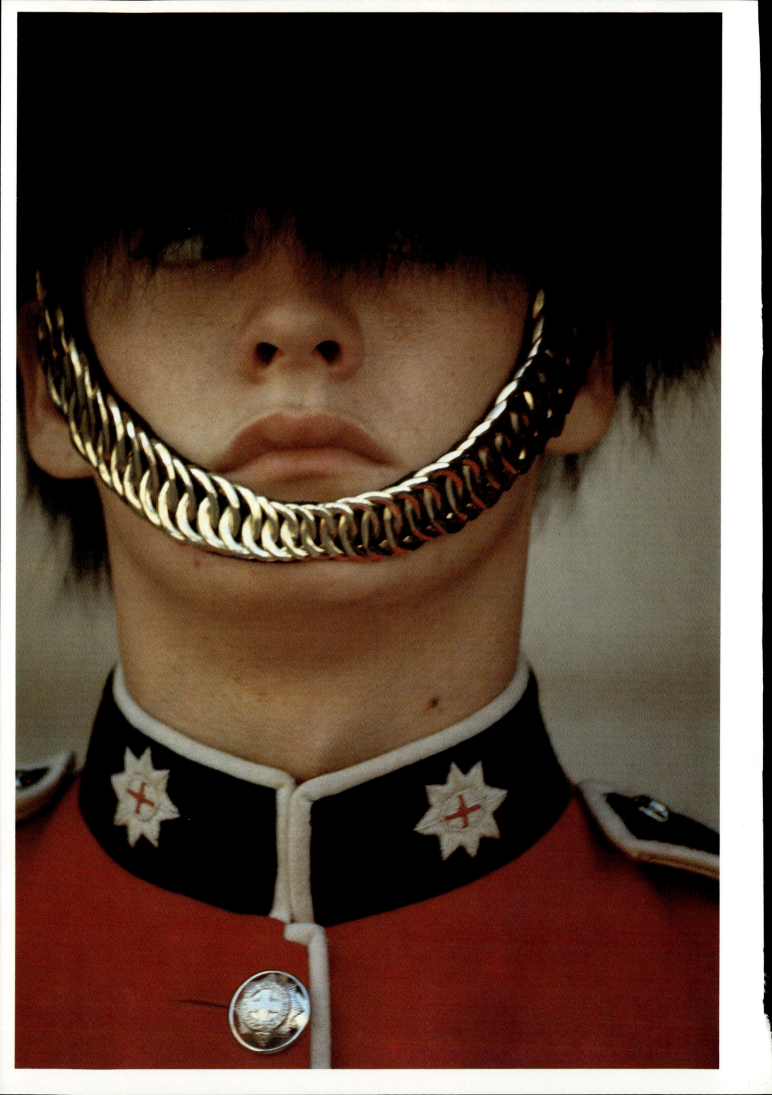

Trooping the Colour at Horse Guards' Parade. This magnificent ceremony happens every year on the Queen's official birthday (in June, when it might not rain) but you won't see the Queen riding her horse again, because of old age — the horse's. The ceremony itself is preceded by a parade along the Mall, when the Queen and her royal entourage ride or travel by royal coach to Horse Guards to inspect her troops.

A young trumpeter, above, in an oversized marine helmet and right, a pensioner at the Royal Hospital, Chelsea, dressed up for a walk along King's Road with the rest of London's masqueraders. Built by Christopher Wren in 1682-92, the hospital houses old and disabled soldiers who are a familiar sight in Chelsea in their scarlet summer uniform and dark blue winter ones.

Following double-page: Royal Tournament at Earl's Court, an armed-forces pageant for the public.

The City Sleeps

One winter's night, I went to Ronnie Scott's, a jazz place in Soho. The jazz at Ronnie Scott's is first rate. There must have been three or four hundred people in there — smoking, drinking, trying to talk, trying to listen, trying to catch a waiter. My friends were having a fine time, but I decided to leave early, alone.

I didn't have a car. Taxis and mini-cabs jammed the streets. Everyone was waving them down, but they were full already. When I arrived at the tube, the grate had been pulled across the entrance. It was closed. I walked down Charing Cross Road, through Trafalgar Square and east, along the Strand. No cabs. In front of Charing Cross Station, two hundred people queued patiently at the taxi rank. No cabs. I walked to a bus stop and squinted at the schedule. The last bus had left twenty minutes earlier; the next wasn't due for an hour. I walked on, still hoping for a cab. At Waterloo Bridge, I turned right and headed over the Thames. On the opposite bank, the pavement ended. I stood on the rim of a deserted junction watching the traffic lights change from green to amber to red, to red and amber, and back to green again. After a long time, a station wagon with a cracked windscreen pulled up beside me. An old man with a ragged beard poked his head out. "You lost?" I explained the problem. He told me to get in. I did, and he drove me home for a fiver. I was in bed by 3 a.m., and I haven't ventured out past midnight again.

Some cities — New York, Naples, Istanbul, Calcutta — were built, I'm sure, over massive underground power generators that keep them rumbling and grinding all day and all night. Those cities don't sleep; London does. It has its cults and its dives and its after-hours clubs. But in the main, London enjoys the homely pleasures. Its shopkeepers, its publicans, its train drivers and its bus drivers all know when to go home. London rests on Sundays. It takes two weeks off at Christmas. It doesn't work too hard. London has its peevish expatriates, me included, who miss those sleepless cities. But I don't know one of us who would get into a strange car with a strange man at 2 a.m. on the wrong side of a lonely bridge, be it Brooklyn or Howrah. And I don't know one of us who won't miss London when it comes time to leave.